IMAGES
of America

NORTHAMPTON

NEW HAVEN AND NORTHAMPTON
DAILY
CANAL BOAT LINE,
AND
STEAMBOAT TO CHEAPSIDE.

The New Haven and Northampton Canal Transportation Line have extended their line of Boats to Cheapside, by adding a Steamboat to run from Northampton. They have also a Steamboat running in connection with the above line from the Basin Wharf in New Haven to New York.

By this arrangement Goods shipped from Albany and Boston by the Western Railroad via Westfield Depot, and from New York and the South via New Haven, will arrive at Cheapside with safety and regularity in the best deck Canal Boats.

The Steamboat Franklin will leave Northampton for Cheapside landing, on MONDAY, WEDNESDAY, and FRIDAY. Returning, leave Cheapside landing on TUESDAY, THURSDAY, and SATURDAY. The Steamboat SALEM will leave the Basin Wharf in New Haven for New York, every MONDAY and THURSDAY at 9 o'clock P. M. Returning leave Old Slip, New York, every TUESDAY and FRIDAY, at 5 o'clock P. M. For freight or passage inquire of J. & N. BRIGGS, No. 40 South Street, New York, or of N. A. BACON, New Haven, or of the Captain on board.

Freight from Boston and Albany will be delivered daily at the Brick Depot, Westfield, and transhipped without delay in the canal boats for Northampton and Cheapside landing, near Greenfield, and in connection with

BEECHER'S DAILY LINE FROM NEW HAVEN,

the present arrangement affords facilities and dispatch hitherto unenjoyed.

The rates of freight generally have been reduced, and Flour from Albany via the Western Railroad, will be delivered at Northampton, *for 34 cents per barrel, and from Albany to Cheapside landing for 40 cents.*

For further particulars inquire at the store house west side of the Deerfield Bridge, at Cheapside, of JOHN R. BOYLE; HENRY BEECHER, New Haven; J. & N. BRIGGS, No. 40 South Street, New York, or of the subscriber at Northampton.

JOSEPH L. KINGSLEY, *General Agent.*

Northampton, April 1, 1845.

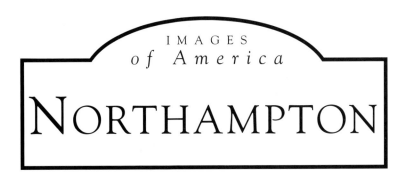

IMAGES of America
NORTHAMPTON

James M. Parsons

First published 1996
Copyright © James M. Parsons, 1996

ISBN 0-7524-0425-3

Published by Arcadia Publishing,
an imprint of the Chalford Publishing Corporation
One Washington Center, Dover, New Hampshire 03820
Printed in Great Britain

Library of Congress Cataloging-in-Publication Data applied for

Contents

Acknowledgments		6
Introduction		7
1.	Always Ready to Serve	9
2.	All Around the Town	23
3.	Taking Care of Business	35
4.	Up in the Morning, Out on the Job	45
5.	Special Events both Good and Bad	71
6.	So Much To Do, So Little Time	79
7.	Home: Where the Heart Is	99
8.	One Last Glance	119

Acknowledgments

The photographs in this volume have been borrowed from the collections of the Forbes Library, the Florence Museum, Historic Northampton, and Raymond LaBarge of Leeds. Recognition and gratitude must be accorded to the artistry and skill of the photographers of Northampton who captured these moments in time. These notably include photographers of the *Daily Hampshire Gazette* over the years and the Howes Brothers, as well as Walter E. Corbin, Robert P. Emrick, Bob Finn, Hardie & Schadee, the Ingraham Brothers, F.N. Kneeland, the Knowlton Brothers, Frank McCarthy, Katherine McClellan, F. Schadee, A.J. Schillaire, and the anonymous others behind the camera.

Introduction

In 2004 Northampton, Massachusetts, will celebrate the 350th anniversary of her settling by a hardy band of pioneers from Connecticut. By the time photography joined with the written word to record the passage of time, Northampton was already two hundred years old with a proud history intimately interwoven with the nation's larger story.

Before there were any devices that preserved images of reality for future generations, this frontier town living under the threat of hostile attack had grown into a place hailed as the "Athens of the Connecticut Valley." To the Swedish Nightingale Jenny Lind, the town was the "Paradise of America." Dr. Josiah Gilbert Holland, author of *Kathrina*, crowned Northampton "Queen village of the meads."

Henry Ward Beecher, in his novel *Norwood*, affirmed that "No finer village glistens in the sunlight, or nestles under arching elms than that which looks over the transcendent valley of the Connecticut . . . how a man could live there and ever get his eyes to the ground, I cannot imagine."

In August of 1847, Charles Sumner said as he stood on Mount Holyoke and looked over the Connecticut River valley below: "I have been all over England, have traveled through the Highlands of Scotland; I have passed up and down the Rhine, have ascended Mount Blanc and stood on the Compagna at Rome; but have never seen anything so surpassingly lovely as this."

The charms of the "Meadow City"—which have also prompted similar tributes in our century—continue to inspire newcomers, visitors, and residents to this day. The seemingly inexhaustible fertility of the meadows remains a marvel to agronomists from around the world. The renaissance of the city's downtown is the model that other New England towns openly envy and hope to emulate. In the *Northampton Book of 1954* that celebrated the city's tercentenary, Northampton was characterized as "A Supremely Likable Town." Natives of our town have always known this as fact. The only difference between then and now is that the secret is out.

This book is not a book about the history of Northampton since the advent of photography. It is a glimpse of a world that is either gone or greatly changed, sometimes beyond recognition, with an occasional more recent picture to remind us of life's continuum. It is a personal glance at the past because the selection of photographs by someone other than the author, from the thousands available, would undoubtedly result in a different view.

Northampton's history is a story of physical blessings, events, and personages beyond comparison with all but a few American communities. In recent years, a three-day event has been held each summer that attracts 60,000 to 80,000 visitors to the community. Called "The Taste of Northampton," it features samples from the varied menus of the dozens of first-rate restaurants that help make today's Northampton such a popular destination. Using a historical rather than a culinary theme, the following is also a "Taste of Northampton"—a sampling of Northampton's remarkable past that may reveal to the reader at least some of the Meadow City's vast appeal.

Much of this history was dictated by physical features of the land. The Connecticut River, the rich meadows it created, and the mountains that overlook it define the region. There is also the Mill River, unlovely in name but generous in the power it provided to the dozens of factories it spawned along its route.

Settlers from Connecticut borrowed the name of an English city in naming Northampton, but to the Native Americans the area was always known as Nonotuck. When peaceful relations with local tribes gave way to more global confrontations, lives were lost throughout the region and citizen soldiers took up arms as they have done ever since when their liberties were threatened and the nation called.

Here witches were accused; Daniel Shays started his rebellion; and the Protestant divine Jonathan Edwards led the Great Awakening. The first million dollar bank robbery took place in Northampton and the Apostle of Bran, Sylvester Graham, lived and died here. Four United States senators rest in the city's Bridge Street Cemetery.

Here the Northampton Association of Education and Industry, a utopian society, found a home; runaway slaves found refuge on their flights to freedom; and philanthropy flowered with the founding of institutions that still prosper and serve after a century's passing.

Here water cures attracted such varied personages as Thomas "Stonewall" Jackson; the infamous Henry Wirz, the only man executed for Civil War crimes; and Alexander Graham Bell, who helped in the establishment of the world famous Clarke School for the Deaf.

Here Sophia Smith realized her dream of founding the women's higher educational institution that we know as Smith College, the largest women's college in the United States, and President Calvin Coolidge rose from being a local common council member and mayor all the way to the White House.

All these memorable contributors and contributions supply only tastes of a truly remarkable city. Enjoy your visit in these pages and experience the reality of a community as ready for the unpredictable future of the twenty-first century as its pioneer settlers were for the challenges of the seventeenth.

James M. Parsons
April 1996

One
Always Ready to Serve

The commitment to doing one's part has always been as fundamental to New Englanders as the work ethic that drives them. This commitment has been manifested in the daily lives of individuals since the settlement of the region. In Northampton, doing one's part could have meant erecting a section of palisade to protect the town, maintaining a road over one's property, drilling with a military company, or paying one's share of the cost of church and clergy. It might also have meant being a member of a firefighting company, providing wood for the stove in your neighborhood school, or joining the "Society for the Detection of Thieves and Robbers." Such community involvement is a spirit that continues to this day, and so this book begins with a salute to all those who have served or continue to serve our nation and our community.

Alfred Crimmi's great mural, painted under government auspices in the 1930s, was removed from its original location in the post office and re-hung in the courthouse. The mural depicts work, religion, and education in the history of Northampton.

Though he rests in Peekskill, NY, where he died on a military expedition, Revolutionary War hero Seth Pomeroy is paid a tribute in the Bridge Street Cemetery in Northampton. Pomeroy turned down the command of the colonial forces at Bunker Hill to fight as a common soldier.

As the band plays and the citizens salute, Civil War veterans of the Grand Army of the Republic march under their swirling colors into Cosmian Hall in Florence for Memorial Day services in 1917.

Edwin L. Olander was a United States Marine Corps Corsair pilot with the Black Sheep Squadron in the South Pacific who earned the status of "Ace" with the downing of five Japanese planes. He was elected mayor upon his return to Northampton.

Captain Geoffrey Olander, grandson of Edwin Olander, continues the tradition of service to our country, as fundamental to living in this valley as breathing its air, tilling its soil, and savoring its natural beauty. Captain Olander is a United States Marine Corps Harrier Jump Jet pilot and the proud father of a son born in 1996 on the anniversary of the Marine Corps' creation.

Members of the Grand Army of the Republic fall in on Memorial Day in 1911. Forty-six years had passed since the Civil War ended with Lee's surrender to Grant in 1865, but GAR numbers were still strong.

Ten million incendiary bombs were produced at the International Silver Company in Florence during World War II. Here, women workers in slacks—with their hair covered and wearing safety goggles or glasses for safety—do additional machining on the rough-cast bombs stacked in the foreground.

In World War II, Smith College was used as a training base for WAVES. Physical conditioning on the college athletic fields was an important element of their program.

During World War II the Prophylactic Brush Company was involved in extensive war production that required tight security. This seventeen-man police force provided coverage twenty-four hours a day at the company's several plants.

Dad's in the army and he's ready too! It seems certain that this picture occupied a special spot in the heart of a proud serviceman in World War II.

Northampton Hook and Ladder and its team of volunteers are in top form in 1879 on the lawn of the courthouse. The public scale is behind the elm trees. In the distance is the intersection of Main and King Streets.

Florence Hose Number 2 company members rally in front of Cosmian Hall in 1880. Fierce competitions with other local volunteer firefighters took place in front of the First Church; the steeple of the church measured the highest stream pumped by each team.

A gleaming new pumper is proudly displayed next door to the fire station in Florence. It must have been an important addition to the department, judging by the overflowing flowers in the stack.

The steamer responds to a fire alarm from the Masonic Street Fire Station in 1914. In the background is city hall, the Unitarian church, and Memorial Hall.

Northampton's grand new hook and ladder truck, labeled "Combination No. 3," stands ready in front of the Masonic Street Fire Station. Behind the truck are the doors through which horses had always dashed with equipment in tow. The horses, the proud firefighters, and the truck are all gone, and the fire station's replacement may finally be on the horizon.

The Florence Post Office was located in the Parsons Block in 1904. The area shown here is now a part of Bird's Store, a Florence landmark.

Mailman William P. Donovan takes a break at the water fountain in the center of Florence, where a cool drink was even made available for man's best friend.

Members of the Northampton Police Department around the turn of the century strike a formidable pose in front of city hall. Mustaches were obviously de rigueur at the time, as only two of the fourteen minions of the law favored a clean upper lip.

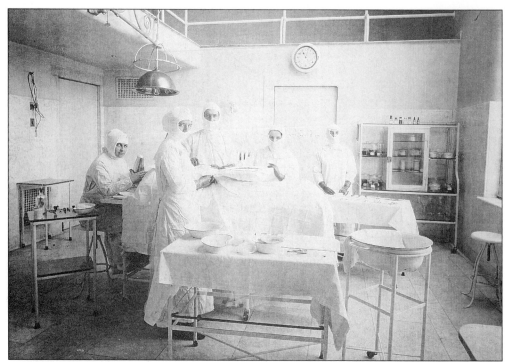

A surgical team at the Cooley Dickinson Hospital prepares to operate in the new Shepherd Surgery wing. Most striking perhaps is the absence of mechanical devices of any kind.

The city infirmary, more commonly known as the "poor house," was built in 1881 on Prospect Street where the synagogue now stands. Subsidized housing for the elderly, the handicapped, and low-income families addressed the infirmary's mission in later years. The building was razed in 1961 by the B'Nai Israel congregation prior to the construction of their new synagogue.

The Cooley Dickinson Hospital of today bears little resemblance to the original of a century ago. The *Gazette* then described in detail the color scheme of the hospital's exterior, which emphasized various earth tones on trim, clapboards, and shingles.

The Wright Home for Young Women on Bridge Street was provided and endowed by the Wright sisters in 1922 as a "home for rest and recuperation for Northampton young women."

The watering of streets was an ongoing effort to keep down dust on dry summer days. This tanker was owned by Gleason Brothers, furniture and piano movers, and had just been filled up from the pipe in front of what became the Rose Tree Inn on Bridge Street.

The years have not diminished its beauty, but no waters flow in the now-arid watering fountain still standing in the center of Florence. This gift to the village by Julius P. Maine was offered as a tribute to his brother and was a popular respite for four-legged creatures of all sizes.

Two
All Around the Town

If Jenny Lind returned to Northampton after a century, she could stand on the steps of city hall, look up or down Main Street, and still recognize the town she loved despite the changes over the years. If she toured the town she would surely be dazzled by Smith College, delighted by the Academy of Music, and impressed by the First Church and courthouse, but saddened by the disappearance of so many grand old homes and buildings that have been replaced in the name of progress. She would wonder at the disappearance of the majestic elms but would still enjoy the warm reception and the natural beauty that brought her back on her honeymoon to her own "Paradise of America."

Shop Row on Main Street is on the left, and the fourth courthouse, built in 1824 and torn down in 1885, is on the right. City hall and Memorial Hall are in the distance.

This is a view of Strong Avenue prior to the building of the railroad overpass in 1897. The Bay State Hotel is on the right and across the street is the Connecticut River Railroad station. The Belding Silk Mill is in the distance, and a Williamsburg trolley stands ready for its journey.

This panoramic view from the corner of Main Street and Strong Avenue looking toward Bridge Street where the railroad overpass stands does not exist today. Beyond the grade crossing built in 1897 is the building that was once an Episcopal church and later the city's first synagogue.

Remove the intrusions of the airport and Interstate Route 91, and Northampton's meadows look today much as they did when the town was settled in 1654. This soil, which was the gift of the Connecticut River, is still the pride of regional agriculturists.

The First National Bank stood at the corner of Main and King Streets when horses still challenged the automobile's place on the road. The building was replaced in 1927 with the Art Deco-style building we are familiar with today. With the demise of the First National Bank, the building became a jewelry store of extraordinary beauty.

The fountain on the lawn in the late 1800s overlooks a very different King Street than the one we know today. The Williston house, the old YMCA, and the O.O. Roberts house appear along its eastern side. The Calvin Theater now occupies the site of the Roberts house.

King Street was still unpaved at the turn of the century, but the YMCA building had electricity and could be accessed by electric trolley from a distance. The chamber of commerce booth and the registry of deeds are located here today.

Remove the cars, wagons, and pre-air-conditioning awnings, and the Main Street of nine decades ago would look much the same as it does today.

Frank Pasano's Columbia Shoe Dressing Parlor at 146 Main Street was barely 8 feet wide, but plenty of advertising was squeezed into its narrow storefront. On the right stood the Hampshire National Bank, or "White Bank," which was having its assets stolen by an employee at the time this picture was taken in the 1920s.

The Jones Block stood on Court Street directly behind the courthouse. This building was replaced by the registry of deeds, and in 1976 the courthouse annex incorporated the registry building into the expanded facility.

The Holley house stood on Main Street along with F.A. Brandle's livery stable next to the Academy of Music. The house and land were acquired for a park to honor Revolutionary War hero Casmir Pulaski in 1906.

The Edwards Church stood across the street from the First Church on the corner of Old South Street. It was destroyed by fire.

Northampton's first Catholic church was located on King Street next to Church Street. When Saint Mary's was completed in 1885, this church was no longer needed. The deceased buried in the churchyard were moved to the new cemetery on Bridge Road.

Isaac Damon was only twenty-eight when he built the First Church, which was dedicated in 1812. It was the fourth meetinghouse and it graced Main Street until it was destroyed by fire in 1876. In 1886, the courthouse on the right was replaced by the building currently in use.

The "Gothic Seminary" was built in 1835 as a school for girls, and after fifteen years it became a school for boys known as "The Collegiate Institute." Next it was a school dedicated to instructing teachers of the deaf For fifteen years after that it was known as "Shady Lawn," an institution for mental patients and alcoholics. In 1891 it became Saint Michael's Parochial School and educated 225 pupils in its first year.

The "Parsons Elm" in front of the Noah Parsons house on Old South Street and its equally majestic neighbors suggest the amount of shade these giants provided at one time. One can picture the arches they created on Bridge and Elm Streets before the great Dutch Elm blight.

The Florence Savings Bank was established in 1873 and was located in the law offices of Henry Herrick Bond on the second floor of the Davis Block. A separate building was completed in 1891.

The proscenium arch above the stage of Cosmian Hall was elaborately painted and bore the motto: "Above All Things, Truth Beareth Away The Victory." The building was erected in 1874 and demolished in 1948. All that remains is the bell, a cornerstone, and color slides of its interior.

The Florence Hotel and the Parsons house, enclosed by the picket fence, no longer exist at the corner of Main and Maple Streets in Florence, nor does the tower of Cosmian Hall, the vantage point for the photographer that took this image. A gas station occupies the hotel site and the Parsons Block dominates the opposite corner.

Three
Taking Care of Business

From its beginnings as a crossroads, county seat, and center of trade, Northampton has had accommodations well-known to the weary traveler. Early taverns such as the Edwards, Warner, Strong, and others were replaced by hotels like the Mansion House, the Draper, Rahar's, the Florence, and the Leeds. Hospitality is still one of the main attractions of modern Northampton. Fine restaurants to suit every taste combine with hotels, motels, and bed-and-breakfast establishments to provide visitors with food, drink, and a retreat from busy days of shopping and sight-seeing, or evenings of entertainment to suit any mood.

The Norwood Hotel stood on the corner of Bridge and Hawley Streets. Calvin and Grace Coolidge spent their wedding night here. The building fell victim to changing economic needs and fire. The post office building now occupies part of the hotel lot.

Hotels

Northampton has four good hotels, many smaller inns and excellent boarding houses of the old fashioned type. In fact, there are accommodations to meet every taste and purse. Owing to the presence of more than 2000 college girls the city also has an unusual number of unique and attractive lunch rooms, tea gardens and restaurants.

This brochure, published in 1930, extols Northampton's hotels; the brand new Hotel Northampton is given star billing.

This rare view of the Mansion House built by Isaac Damon was taken from the tower of College Hall in 1879. The Mansion House occupied the site of Saint Mary's Church on Elm Street. Sparsely settled State Street had been the location of the canal connector to the Connecticut River.

Clark's Ferry tollhouse and inn stood at the corner of Damon Road and Bridge Street until the coming of Route 91. The building was dismantled and moved to Bay Road in Hadley, where it was reassembled and beautifully restored.

The Round Hill Hotel (c. 1877) was the site of the water cure that attracted such southern luminaries before the Civil War as Thomas J. "Stonewall" Jackson. Near the tree is Edith Childs and "little white Topsy."

Built in 1896 as Century Hall, a Smith College dormitory, this building became the Plymouth Hotel a year later. It stood at the corner of West and Green Streets across from Forbes Library and was torn down in 1931.

Dr. Munde's Water Cure on the banks of the Mill River in Florence was popular with patients from the South in pre-Civil War days. Dr. Munde's strong Union sentiments drove away his southern clientele by the outset of the war in 1861.

The famed Rose Tree Inn on Bridge Street was started when Madame Anna de Naucaze bought the two-hundred-year-old building in 1909. The enterprise lasted until 1923 and today the building is a tire store. The handsome saltbox next door has been well maintained over the years and is still one of the city's finest historical homes.

The Florence Hotel, once the Florence House, was a busy establishment on the corner of Main and Maple Streets that expanded in later years to a three-story building. The horse-drawn trolley ran between 1866 and 1893, connecting busy Florence center with downtown Northampton.

The Moody Tavern, also known as Edwards' Tavern, once sat in Robert's Meadow on the corner of Chesterfield and Sylvester Roads. It was built in 1773, and burned on July 4, 1924. The tavern was located at the beginning of the Albany Turnpike and served as a tollhouse. The Marquis de LaFayette stopped here on his tour through Massachusetts in 1825.

The Strong Tavern and Charles Lee's laundry stood on the corner of Main and North Maple Streets in Florence. The tavern was built in 1809 and operated until the coming of the railroads in 1843.

Solomon Warner's Tavern in Leeds stood opposite the intersection of Florence Street and Route 9. In stagecoach times it was a popular stop. When the Bear Hill property was purchased for a U.S. Veterans' Hospital, the building was razed.

The Leeds Hotel was located on the corner of Water Street and the Hotel Bridge. It is difficult to picture this large, handsome building and its equally large barn on the small lot it occupied on the river's edge.

The horse-drawn North Farms school bus is shown here in 1935 on North Maple Street in Florence. The building in the background housing Roger's Store was demolished to provide more parking space.

The handsome Leeds Hotel succumbed to fire, but the Hotel Bridge still stands just above the second of the four dams along the Mill River. The once-deep river, which powered the mills along its banks, is now filled with silt and the water is less than knee deep.

Livery stables like C.H. Burnham's in Florence were the Hertz and Avis of the pre-automobile era. Burnham's, on Depot Street, became Gagnon & Forsander's Garage which, like so many other similar businesses, made the transition to servicing automobiles.

43

A patient pup has all the comforts of home as he waits for his master to finish his meal inside.

Four
Up in the Morning, Out on the Job

Going off to work today in Northampton is vastly different in many ways from what it was in earlier eras. The Mill River in years gone by was lined with factories whose power came from the river, whose labor was supplied by workers who usually lived within walking distance, and whose hours of operation were typically from dawn to dark six days a week. Farming was the other chief means of earning one's bread, but the appeal of "short" working hours in the factories enticed some young people off the land. There were also the merchants of Main Street, whose goods were typically and intentionally both homely and practical, characterizations the vendors would have regarded as compliments. Service occupations were in their infancy. How far they were to come is suggested by the "Lunatic Asylum" on the hill and Cooley Dickinson's hospital, established to provide health care for the "worthy poor."

These men were the industrial movers and shakers of the last half of the nineteenth century in Florence and Leeds. The best known are Alfred T. Lilly and Samuel L. Hill (first and second from the left in the front row) and Lucius Dimock (on the right in the back row).

It is hard for today's supermarket generations to picture how many little neighborhood stores once served residents. This one at 245 Bridge Street was typical of the small grocery stores scattered around the city one hundred years ago.

Chancey Frayer ran this store and gas station on the corner of Main and Chestnut Streets in Florence in 1918. Pan Am gas was 20¢ and 23¢ cents a gallon, and LaSalle's popular ice cream was available inside.

The building on the corner of Main and North Maple Streets in Florence has served many purposes over the years. In 1904, O'Donnell Groceries and The Lilly Theater occupied the ground floor overlooking a muddy Main Street.

In 1908 a young clothier named Ralph Levy decided to try selling his wares in Northampton for three weeks. His store lasted sixty-eight years. Mr. Levy is shown here picking the winner of a new television in the early 1950s with Bernard Riley in a chamber of commerce promotion.

In the 1930s, Aubrey Butler, of Butler and Ullman Florists, began shipping roses by plane from LaFleur Airport.

The E.J. Gare & Son Jewelry Store opened in 1785 and closed in 1994. The Gare name was associated with the business since 1884. A superb collection of signage, tools, parts, and artifacts of all kinds—some two centuries old—was donated to Historic Northampton by the Gare-Polachek family.

This unusual staging was devised in 1893 to assist in the conversion from horse-drawn to electric trolleys. Perhaps the fancy headdress on the horse was meant to prevent him from observing the newfangled gadget that would soon put him in the unemployment line!

This trolley from Northampton to Florence is pictured on Main Street in 1890 in front of the Polly Pomeroy house, the site now occupied by the Masonic Block.

This trolley from Northampton to Florence followed State and Prospect Streets. The summertime open trolleys were popular cool rides on hot summer evenings.

On the 100th birthday of Densella Johnson in August of 1905, John C. Hammond gave her a trolley trip to Mount Tom. Mr. Hammond is standing on the running board next to her.

The large stores on King Street today give no indication that there was, for almost one hundred years, a large freight yard on their site—complete with sidetracks, switches, turntables, and freight houses. In this building the operators kept track of all the railroad cars and engines as they were shuttled around the yard.

This was the freight station of the New York, New Haven & Hartford Railroad in the King Street rail yards. The men on the left with the hand trucks would unload freight into the depot, where it would be processed by the staff and readied for pickup by the freight movers on the right.

Only Charles H. Hayden Jr., in the first row on the left, is identified in this picture of Adams Express Company workers at the railroad express office at Northampton's rail yards.

Charlie LaFountain and Archie Marcotte of Leeds are ready to deliver groceries and fish for Archie's brother, Sidney Marcotte, who operated a grocery store on Water Street in Leeds.

A load of lumber passes by the unique "round house" on Conz Street around the turn of the century. Until the rerouting of the Mill River and the building of the dike system, this area was prone to flooding.

A familiar face to older residents of Leeds is Warren "Bub" Tower, who delivered milk from his dairy farm on Haydenville Road throughout the village. Now a hardy ninety-three years old, "Bub" no longer delivers milk but is as lively as he was in those days when no Fourth of July was complete without a firecracker's explosion announcing his arrival.

It's a busy day at the blacksmith's shop on Merrick Lane where, it seems, all the customers want their horses shod at the same time.

In the late 1890s, Hyde's Violin Factory operated at 80 Parsons Street. As the small building suggests, this was a modest "factory," but there was nothing modest about the quality of a Hyde instrument.

Oscar Clark is shown here at work on violins and other stringed instruments in various stages of manufacture and repair in the Hyde Violin Factory around 1900.

The S.E. Bridgman Bookstore was a fixture on Main Street for decades. It was staffed around 1890 by, from left to right: E.H. Lyman, A.G. Thompson, Annie C. Bridgman, Annie P. Palmer, and proprietor S.E. Bridgman.

Bernache and O'Brien's Barber Shop in the Parsons Block in Florence served generations of village residents. It was a classic old-time barber shop with massive chairs, paper rollers on headrests, one's own shaving mug, and fragrances guaranteed to make the freshly shorn irresistible!

These young women were all mill workers living in the Nonotuck Silk Mill Boarding House around 1885. The owners of New England factories took seriously their responsibility to provide for the morals as well as health of their young female workers.

The paternalistic factory owners of the nineteenth century provided housing for many of their workers. The Nonotuck Silk Mill Boarding House for women stood on the corner of Pine and Corticelli Streets in Florence.

At the end of the day in the dye house of the Nonotuck Silk Company, the vats were discharged into the Mill River. In one of her incomparable articles on local history, Alice Manning recalled the fascinating, swirling colors that drifted down the stream as the factory approached closing time.

The spooling room at the Nonotuck Mill was well-lit and protected by a sprinkler system, but the belt-driven machines still made it a dangerous work setting. In an era before health insurance, it is chilling to think of the futures of families whose chief wage earners were the victims of the catastrophic injuries reported in the *Gazette*.

The Florence Hotel gave way to service stations on the corner of Main and Maple Streets in the village center. The popular John Breguet ran the station when this photograph was taken on a beautiful summer day in 1946.

The Sheffield Fox Farm in Florence raised prize foxes during the 1920s. The animals were so valuable that a guard tower was necessary to protect them from thieves. Fur's decline in popularity ended the enterprise.

The original building of the Florence Manufacturing Company was finished in 1867 and produced brushes, lockets, daguerreotype cases, and buttons. This building has been enclosed on three sides by additions.

The Florence Manufacturing Company succeeded A.P. Critchlow & Company. Florence Manufacturing had expanded its facilities four times and adopted "The Pro-phy-lac-tic Brush Company" as its name when this picture was taken at the turn of the century.

George LaFlam of the Norwood Engineering Company in Florence looks like Charlie Chaplin in the film *Modern Times* next to the massive gear.

The building housing the Nonotuck Silk Mill and I.S. Parsons' store in its right half is still standing on Nonotuck Street with ProCorp now occupying the space.

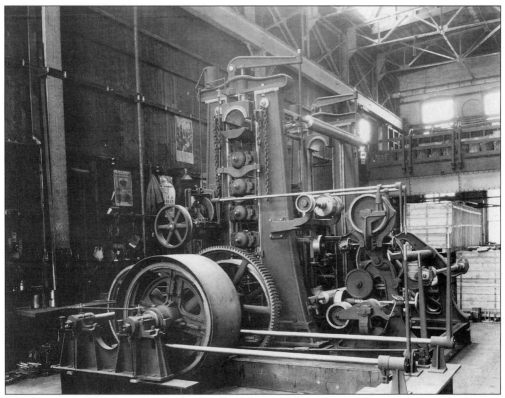

The function of this massive machine at the Norwood Engineering Company is unknown, but the period of its use is suggested by the *Magazine of the War* on the wall. The cover appears to depict Admiral Dewey during the Spanish-American War.

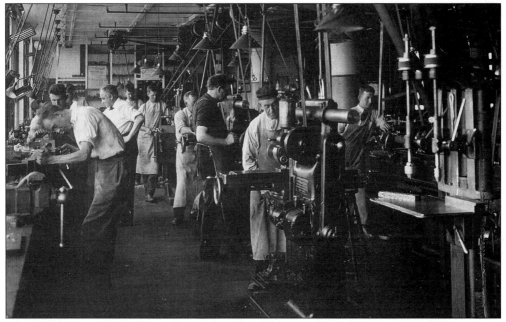

This image shows the machine shop at the Pro-phy-lac-tic Brush Company (c. 1905).

In 1889, Dr. W. Learned raised four to five hundred hogs at a time on his Strawberry Hill farm. "No Cholera Here" was the Strawberry Hill Pork trademark that quieted the public's fear of the deadly disease.

The hay crop on A.T. Lilly's Spring Street lot on June 28, 1880, was a record breaker. Four tons per acre were taken from the fertile fields of Broughton's Meadows.

Those strange-looking devices in the area's cucumber fields are affectionately known as "Hadley B-52's." These young workers dubbed their winged but flightless craft the "SS Enterprise."

The process of raising tobacco in the valley has changed little since it was introduced. Once a mainstay of the agricultural community, tobacco had virtually disappeared as a crop until recently. The growing popularity of cigar smoking has prompted farmers to convert some fields and harvest the crop once again.

The workers at Bartlett's Saw Mill in the late 1880s would be right at home in today's logging industry, but they would be amazed at the equipment used by their modern counterparts.

These laborers at the stone quarry on North King Street (c. 1890) might well be mistaken for the '49ers on the other side of the continent. Quarries were scattered around town, since there was no shortage of stone in our area and moving giant blocks of it was a task best achieved over short distances.

This brickyard and sawmill was located on West Street in 1873. Samuel Day is pictured without a vest or coat. Another major brickyard was located on the flats between Elm and North Elm Streets.

In 1899 these cutlery workers at the Clement Company in the Bay State section of town operated grinding and polishing machines under grim working conditions.

The Belding Brothers Silk Mill stood on Hawley Street next to the railroad tracks. In 1902, six hundred workers were employed here. Belding's was the largest silk producer in the world, with mills located across the U.S. and Canada.

Maynard's Hoe Shop, which stood at the end of Green Street on the Mill River, was built in 1866 and partially burned in 1887. The tower and building were removed in 1914–15 and the bricks were used for the Smith College laundry.

The Hockanum Ferry across the Connecticut River provided one of the rare circumstances in which horses took a ride and man had to provide the power to move.

The old met the new when this 1921 Franklin Sedan, with an air-cooled engine, was being delivered to Northampton from Syracuse, New York, and chanced upon a team of oxen.

This model of the world-famous Florence Sewing Machine—manufactured in Florence in the last century—is on display in the Smithsonian Institution in Washington.

Five
Special Events both Good and Bad

Rivers are a mixed blessing. At their most benign they provide beauty, a means of transportation, power, rich land, water, and food. At their calamitous worst, they can kill and destroy. The Connecticut and Mill Rivers have shown both faces. Dams, dikes, and other flood controls have largely tamed the Connecticut, and it is hard to believe that the tranquil little stream called the Mill River once killed over 140 people in a matter of minutes when a poorly constructed dam gave way. We have also had major bank robberies perpetrated by bank employees and professional thieves from afar, as well as hurricanes and other rebukes from Mother Nature. But mostly, however, we have had wonderful events to celebrate. The reunion of Smith College classes is a rite of spring that reminds us of how loved and beautiful our community is. Anniversaries like the tercentenary celebration, welcome-home parades for servicemen and women, annual observances like Memorial Day and the Three County Fair, and the dedications of facilities remind one that in the Pioneer Valley every day can be a special event.

The Mill River Button Company burned in 1870 and was replaced with this factory in 1872. Just two years later, the Mill River Flood of 1874 killed a number of the workers posing here, destroyed the mills, and swept the bridge away. When the alarm sounded, only minutes remained to reach the safety of the railroad track halfway up the hill in the back.

The Nonotuck Silk Mill in Leeds Center survived the Mill River Flood of 1874, but the bridge and the Nonotuck Silk Mill Boarding House did not. Workers in the mill who stayed in the building were safe, but some of those who ran across the metal bridge toward high ground lost their lives.

The stone bridge on Main Street in Leeds survived the Mill River Flood of 1874, as did the house and the school just beyond it. Workers found several bodies buried in the debris hurled against the bridge. Of the twenty-six bridges that spanned the Mill River from Williamsburg to Northampton, only two were left standing after the flood.

The scoured center of Leeds after the Mill River Flood of 1874 illustrates how fickle Mother Nature can be. The house and the mill were never touched by the torrent that killed and destroyed all in its path just feet away.

The Leeds School on Main Street sustained damage from the Mill River Flood of 1874 and was used as a temporary morgue for its victims. The building was restored as a two-family house that was occupied until it was completely washed away by a freshet on December 10, 1878.

The Corticelli Silk Company float in the 250th anniversary parade featured "oriental" maidens in silk kimonos with parasols, Japanese lanterns, and even a Japanese flag.

Everyone on lower Main Street joined in the celebration of Northampton's 250th anniversary in June of 1904.

The staff of Boyden's popular restaurant on Main Street is ready for a parade, possibly the grand celebration of the end of World War I.

Northampton celebrates the end of the "war to end all wars" with a victory parade up Main Street on November 12, 1918. The balconies of the Draper Hotel provided some of the best locations for viewing the march.

"They don't build them like they used to." In November of 1929, this handsome new Cord front-wheel drive sedan slammed into the Connecticut River Bridge and knocked it off its foundation.

The flood of March 18, 1936, inundated communities all along the Connecticut. Its extraordinary peak reached the road level of the bridges between Northampton and Hadley.

The "Burgy Bullet" lies derailed on its side in Haydenville. Though good-naturedly maligned in its later years, the railroad to the Williamsburg Depot made four daily passenger runs—on time—in its heyday.

This tunnel through the snow piled on Main Street is proof that the Blizzard of '88 was as bad as the records show. On the other side of the street from this vantage point in front of the Draper Hotel is the ill-fated White Bank. Old South Street is on the right.

The laying of the new courthouse cornerstone in 1886 was a big event. The popularity and influence of fraternal orders like the Masons are evident in the numbers of participants wearing aprons and other regalia.

After the Mill River Flood of 1874, a new Cook's Dam in Leeds was built. The large area above the dam is now filled with silt, so only a small remnant of the broad stream that once flowed there exists; the water is only as deep as the cap blocks.

Six
So Much To Do, So Little Time

One might expect that long hours of manual labor on the job in the nineteenth century would have forced worn-out workers to head for the couch in their few free hours. In reality, before the advent of cable television and the Internet, every community was a beehive of recreational activities. There were dozens of clubs, organizations, and fraternities for male and female alike. These groups were based on such themes as religion, nationality, neighborhood, and special interests like baseball, croquet, cycling, canoeing, dramatics, music, or literature (the literary Fortnightly Club is still active after over a century). It is ironic that our lives have become increasingly insulated in an era when the average person has more free time than ever before.

In this 1911 pageant held at "Wildwood" (now Child's Park), the menacing Indian on the left is actually President-to-be Calvin Coolidge. Mrs. Coolidge is third from the right with son John standing in front of her.

It's a leisurely summer ride across the Connecticut River on the Hockanum Ferry for all but the ferry operator. The Summit House and the cable railway can be seen on the mountain in the background.

The paddle-wheel steamer *Mount Holyoke* carried visitors across the Connecticut River, where they were shuttled by stagecoach to the enclosed cable railway and given the ride of their lives to the Summit House on top of the mountain.

The often-overloaded "Talley Ho" stagecoach service to Mount Holyoke had plenty of room remaining on this day in 1896.

These picnickers on Mount Holyoke in 1889 include Mary Edwards, Frank Clark, Harry Williams, Charles Williams, and Mrs. Nellie French Collins.

The lower Leeds Reservoir has always been a popular swimming hole. This large crowd was seeking a respite from the heat on July 2, 1955, in what was then called the "baby end of the res." Only the distant area, known as the David Musante Beach, is now used for swimming.

The brush shop dam in Florence may not have had the purest waters but nobody seemed to mind on hot days in the 1940s. This was the site of the first settlement in what was called Broughton's Meadow, where the first dam powered a sawmill and an oil mill.

Skating was once a popular winter pastime on the Mill River. Here in Leeds around 1903–1906 over one hundred well-dressed skaters enjoy the stretch under the Hotel Bridge.

Skating on Arcanum Field was still popular in 1957 when the city's recreation department was able to flood outdoor areas around the city.

Warner Oland, the big screen's first Charlie Chan, married Edith Shearn of Leeds and summered there for years. Shown here in 1921, Oland was an ardent golfer and tennis player and once won the Northampton Country Club's Handicap Championship.

There was little room left for the water in the summer of 1933 when the new Look Park Pool was stormed by eager swimmers. The scratchy wool swimsuits then in use were an unforgettable experience.

Look Park Manager Foss Narum looked after the finest new park and swimming pool in New England in 1933. His lifeguards were, from left to right: Edward Farrell, John Goodrow, Agnes Ryan, Allan Ryan, and Joe Fogg.

The legendary meat-market proprietor Julius Maine of North Maple Street does not look impressed with the mode of transportation chosen by the six passengers in the Model-T. In the background is the railroad grade warning sign and the gate and driveway to the Dr. J. Learned estate, now partly occupied by Forsander Apartments.

The Northampton High School Class of 1912 visits Washington on March 31, 1912. Chaperones are Major Beckman (in the front seat) and Mrs. Calvin Coolidge (in the third).

Ready for a trip to the golf course in their 1931 Chevrolet Phaeton are Doris, Barbara, Arlene, and Ruth Jager.

The legendary George Bean, the "Yankee Auctioneer," practiced his craft successfully from 1913 to 1965. The Friday evening auctions in his backyard were a social event as well as sale. He is shown here on his block while the popular Charlie Stark checks with the cashier.

Northampton Wheel Club members Herbert Graves, Eugene Davis, and Louis L. Campbell pose around 1888. Davis' bicycle is of an advanced design with a unique propulsion system and hand brakes.

The clothes are different but the frog-jumping is the same as it was in the last century. Phillip Judd uses a feather to encourage his frog to jump. Urging the frog to put out his best effort are Phillip's mother Linda and brother Albert.

"Dutch" Robbins, the national marble champion in 1925, wows the locals with a demonstration of his prowess at Smith's School on a chilly April 17, 1926.

The Smith College Class of 1884 is shown here in front of College Hall.

Elfie Whitney, Margie Scheljhnig, and Ethel Hammond sport the proper attire and equipment as they visit the Mammoth Cave in Kentucky in 1907 with guide Josh.

The latest swimwear of a century ago left little to sunburn and much to the imagination. With such a burden of fabric, the very act of swimming must have been a challenge, even to the most athletic woman.

Victorian parlors may be considered cluttered by today's standards, but they had a welcoming, comfortable look as well. Window shutters were functional and kept out the heat or regulated the light during a pleasant afternoon at the easel.

The drum corps of the Corticelli Silk Company of Leeds is ready to march at the 250th anniversary celebration in 1904. The famous kitten and spool of thread trademark adorns the bass drums. Competition among the drum corps representing local industries was keen.

Competition between the city's neighborhoods and industries prevailed in every aspect of life including the volunteer fire departments, sports teams, and musical organizations like the drum corps, whose units were sponsored by organizations and businesses.

Dick Newcomb and his "Masters of Modern Melody" were the most popular big band in the area during the 1920s. Butler "Butch" Gilman (far right) was the last surviving member of this classy musical organization. He was in his nineties when he passed on in July of 1996.

John Charlebois points to a class of Smith College students who received instruction from his father in 1918 at the home of his employer, Alvin Clapp, at 70 Old South Street. Amelia Earhart, who went on to become the world's most famous aviatrix before her death on a round-the-world trip, attended the school with her sister.

On August 9, 1919, two hydroplanes were anchored in the Connecticut River. The number of boaters suggests that this may have been near one of the popular canoe clubs.

"Nine Crows In A Tree" is the name given to this unique gathering by the participants themselves. Maybe watching football on television on a cold fall afternoon isn't such a bad pastime after all.

These drugstore cowboys in front of Whitney's Drug Store in Florence favored straw boaters, but their dark outfits look drab indeed compared to the swell on the right, resplendent in a pork-pie hat and a suit that would allow him to fit right in with "zoot-suiters" of the 1940s.

In the late 1940s, Sid Montague of Westhampton showed three of his Guernseys at the Three County Fair. Sid was as adept at selecting pretty farm hands to display his animals as he was at raising his prize-winning livestock.

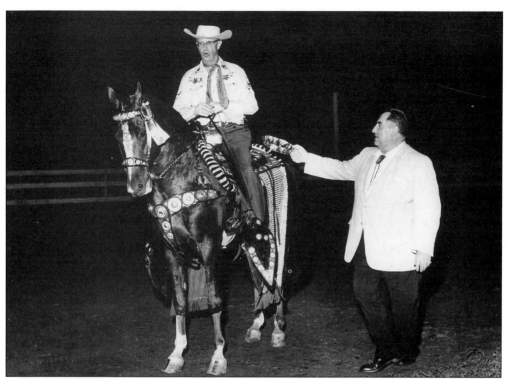

First prize in the parade stallions division of the 1960 Morgan Horse Show, held at the Three County Fairgrounds, is presented by well-known Northampton restaurateur Jack August.

The Lawton brothers of Williamsburg are shown here getting the most out of their team in the 1952 Three County Fair Horse Pulling Contest.

This stork, with its precious cargo, has been sitting on the maternity wing of Cooley Dickinson Hospital for decades. It has played a major role in the explanations given to generations of children regarding the origin of their new brothers and sisters.

Seven
Home:
Where the Heart Is

Typically, the town that transports us back to another era because it looks just the same as it did in the "old days" does not have an active business district and has not been subjected to the demands of growth. Northampton has lost much of its architectural history because of different attitudes toward growth in times past and the demands of an expanding world-famous institution like Smith College. Nine of the first ten houses pictured in this section no longer exist, having been victims of the wrecker's ball. The tenth, the William Parsons house, left the town to grace a street in Darien, Connecticut, in 1937. Even Princeton University has one of Northampton's grandest homes, the stately Greek Revival Sheldon house, which was removed in 1866. The miracle is that, despite this "Paradise Lost," so much beauty and history remains.

The Polly Pomeroy house stood on Main Street next to Smith Charities. It was razed for the construction of the Masonic building that dominates the lower north side after the railroad crossing.

The Dwight house, built by Major Timothy Dwight in 1751 on King Street, was a gambrel-roofed dwelling similar to others around the town; like those others, it was destroyed in the name of progress.

The Solomon Stoddard house on Elm Street stood next to Smith College's chemistry lab and was demolished to make way for the Alumnae House.

The Edwards house on King Street was affectionately known as the "Red Castle." Its appearance hinted at the grace and beauty of a typical Charleston, South Carolina, home. A national grocery chain destroyed it for a new building. Today one can only bank or have an ice cream cone where this special home once stood.

The house of Lieutenant William Parsons was built on Bridge Street in 1754 as an addition to the Captain John Parsons homestead (built in the late 1600s). The Parsons house was disassembled in 1937 and moved to Darien, Connecticut, where it still stands.

The Bowers Mansion on Prospect Street was Ithiel Towne's masterpiece that he designed and built in 1825. In 1904 the Polish community bought it and converted it to a church. With only slight modifications, the house sat 470 worshippers. It was torn down in 1915.

Like the "Red Castle" on King Street, the David Damon house on Bridge Street was sacrificed to make room for a grocery store. The building's last use was as a home for the Knights of Columbus.

Builders and homeowners were enthusiastic about the Greek Revival style, judging by the number of structures bearing reference to it all over the community. Though more modest in overall dimensions than many, the A.O. Skilton house on the corner of Park and King Streets displayed the classic proportions of this style.

The Bodman house stood on Elm Street at the corner of Round Hill Road. The house was acquired and destroyed by Smith College and the site became home to the Helen Hills Chapel.

John Whittelsey, treasurer of the Northampton National Bank, owned this home at 184 Elm Street on January 25, 1876, when it was overrun by a gang of thieves who tied and gagged the residents before stealing over one million dollars from the bank.

Fanny Burr Look, who gave Look Park to the citizens of Northampton, is pictured here in her wedding gown on October 20, 1880.

It doesn't seem likely that Harry E. Carlisle would be out hunting in the woods in his Sunday best.

W. Bristow Bingham is shown here in the rocker; Bradford B. Bingham is holding his favorite toy horse.

In this 1896 Lyman family portrait, E.H.R. Lyman, who gave the Academy of Music to Northampton, is seated second from the right in the front yard of the Lyman Fort Hill Estate on South Street.

The seven Porter children display their "best bib and tucker" around 1905. Standing in front are Mary and Emily, with Harriet and Raymond in the cart. In the back row are Mildred, Wayland, Bennett, and Elizabeth.

This house at 116 North Maple Street in Florence—photographed as part of the Howes Brothers series—stands out from its neighbors because of its distinctive styling. Its tower and mansard roof, with rounded windows projecting into the canted roof line, are elegant touches usually reserved for much larger homes.

Spreadwing, the home of the Mahar family at 4 Park Street in Florence, was built in the late 1860s by businessman Isaac Parsons. The elegance of the era is reflected in the handsome belvedere, the stone greyhounds guarding the stairs, and the rich variety of plantings.

The brick boarding house in the center of Leeds replaced the one destroyed in the Flood of 1874. The large building on the right survived; living or dying during the flood depended on how far up those stairs one could struggle.

After a hundred years this home on Kennedy Road is still recognizable. These residents pose in a fashion typical of the time, when possessions were trotted out and one's best outfit was usually worn for the big event.

In the 1890s, Water Street in Leeds was the area of the village favored by French Canadian immigrants who came to work in the mills. When the Howes Brothers came to take pictures, all were dressed in their very best clothing.

Large families were the norm on Water Street in Leeds among the French Canadians who settled there. The factory in the background to the right is on the other side of Mill River on Main Street.

The classically beautiful Greek Revival James house on Gothic Street, built in 1850, is pictured around 1967, when it housed the Young Women's City Club and Children's Aid and Family Service.

Shown in this c. 1865 photograph are, from left to right: Judge Samuel F. Lyman, Fannie Brewer (standing), Mrs. Lyman, Mrs. Elizabeth Lyman (in the doorway), and Hannah Brewer and Mary Lyman (in the foreground).

In the elegant era before the turn of the century, this reception at 10 Prospect Street was held in the garden of Alexander McCallum, president of McCallum Hosiery.

The Hezekiah Hutchins house was moved around 1839 from Bridge Street to Cherry Street, traveling cross-lots to its new location. An Episcopal church was built on its original site on Bridge Street. In 1905 the church was sold and became Northampton's first synagogue.

These young, barefooted girls stand in front of one of the city's architectural curiosities. The "round house" at 32 Conz Street was built in 1829 by Seth Strong to better take advantage of the sun's rays and prevailing winds.

Martha P. Whitmarsh was photographed reading to Ruth H. Andrews in an old-fashioned kitchen at 107 North Maple Street in Florence.

This gambrel-roof cottage at 252 Bridge Street was a century old when the Howes Brothers photographed it around 1900. It later earned a degree of fame as the Rose Tree Inn, but fell on hard times as a gas station and tire outlet.

Although near duplicates of this 1880s house still exist in the Bridge Street area, few retain its prodigious decorative bracketry or "gingerbread." The prospect of scraping and repainting the cornice brackets alone must have sent later owners looking for a crowbar after a few tries!

Miss Anna May Wallace is surrounded by her favorite toys in Florence in 1889.

The beautiful children of Minna Sullivan Flynn, a graduate of the Class of 1908, Clarke School for the Deaf.

The Collins brothers would certainly have won any "Dapper Lads" contest held in the mid-1880s. Tom and Dick were twins born in 1880. We can only speculate that their older brother was named "Harry."

Eight
One Last Glance

These last pages offer a final look over the shoulder at these moments in time. While the last picture in the book is from our more recent past, for many it represents an era when one's relationships with church, family, employer, community, and nation allowed for the hope that the wrongs in our political, social, and economic systems would ultimately be identified and humanely corrected. The young women in that picture are visiting a furniture store to claim a hope chest, the foundation of a pre-nuptial tradition that is no longer in favor. Though the interest of brides-to-be in a hope chest may have waned over the years, "hope" itself remains immutable, indestructible, and every bit as eternal as it was said to have been when the earliest of the pictures in this book was taken. To those who judge us and our lives as images from their past some hundred years hence we pass on that legacy of hope.

The gentle meandering of the Connecticut and the lush meadowlands of Sunderland, Hadley, and Hatfield are viewed from Mount Sugarloaf looking south to where Mount Holyoke and Mount Tom divide on the horizon.

The Florence Post Office was established in 1852. Before that time, Florence mail was placed in the mailbox of Samuel L. Hill in Northampton, and he brought it to the village each day. In 1891 the post office was located on Maple Street.

George Hayes, Florence's first permanent fireman, shows off his dappled team and firefighting rig on Maple Street.

The men of the Nonotuck Fire Company stand ready in front of the old courthouse in July of 1878. This is the corner of Main and King Streets, where the first agricultural fairs were held. On the right are the Fairbanks scales that were available for public use.

The year is 1926 and only minor rubble sits on the lot soon to be the home of the Hotel Northampton.

After the fire of 1876 that destroyed the First Church, the Northampton Institution for Savings constructed this handsome building between the new stone First Church and the courthouse. In 1915, the institution's structure was replaced by the building now occupied by Fleet Bank.

Little remains today from this view, which was captured from the South Street Bridge c. 1890. The railroad is gone, the Mill River has been diverted, and the dam and bridge have been removed.

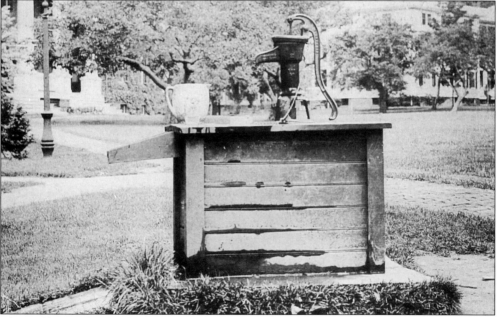

This well, complete with pump, pitcher, and glass, awaited Smith College students near the Dewey house on campus in the mid-1880s. It was a popular stop on a warm spring day.

Jerry LaBarge of Water Street in Leeds displays a pickerel caught in Mill River. With silt now filling the river bed, the river is little more than a foot deep, leaving little room for fish of this size.

The "Burgy Bullet," as the train to Williamsburg was affectionately known, is taking on passengers at the depot in the center of Leeds, which had been completely rebuilt since the Mill River Flood of 1874. The sign advertises P.T. Barnum's last showing of the "Dog Faced Man, Greatest Of All Living Curiosities."

John Ross' store and home were on Yankee Hill's Front Street in Leeds. Mederic Bachand is on the delivery wagon. Clerk Wilfred LeDuc stands next to Miss Ross, Mrs. Ross, and John Ross (owner). Four other groceries in Leeds competed for housewives' business until well after World War II.

The clubhouse of the Northampton Country Club was built in Leeds on land formerly owned by the Nonotuck Silk Company, after members of the Warner Meadow Golf Club grew impatient for a lease extension in 1908. The old course is now Look Park and this clubhouse was replaced with a new building in 1970.

The Butler and Ullman greenhouses stood on Prospect Street between Massasoit Street and Woodlawn Avenue. Today this site is occupied by the Hampshire Regional YMCA.

Hebert Brothers Coal Company had reason to be proud of their gleaming new truck, complete with carriage lamps and a bulb-powered air horn. The building in the background is the Easthampton Town Hall.

Bill Forknall and Ray Casler are in the cab of the Florence Casket Shop's Reo truck at the garage of Frank S. Parsons on Conz Street. The truck is loaded with caskets and containers. The Reo symbol is still visible on the brick wall after almost seventy-five years and the Florence Casket Company is still prospering after nearly 123 years of operation.

In November of 1932, the Northampton Kiwanis Club decided that "enough was enough" and conducted a mock burial of "Old Man Depression" in Look Park.

In the 1950s, girls in high school graduating classes were invited to local furniture stores to receive free, miniature, cedar-lined hope chests; the hope on the store owners' part was that the young women would soon be back to buy the full-sized real thing!